The Boy They

A Memoir of Survival, Truth, and Becoming Myself

by Tremaine Criner

Introduction

"This Story Is For the Ones Who Weren't Supposed to Make It"

If you picked up this book, there's a good chance you've already survived some things people don't talk about out loud.

Maybe you grew up faster than you wanted to.

Maybe you've had authority lie on you, hurt you, or fail you.

Maybe your hunger was bigger than your options.

Maybe you've loved people who didn't know how to love you back.

Maybe you've tried to change your life, only to have your past thrown in your face over and over again.

Or maybe you don't know exactly what you're looking for—you just know you can't keep living the way you've been living.

This book is my story.

But I didn't write it just to tell you what happened to me.

I wrote it to tell you what's possible for you.

You're not holding a polished "from struggle to success" fairy tale.

You're holding the real thing.

The grief. The hunger. The violence. The love. The wrecks. The rebuilding.

You'll read about jail cells and juvenile centers.

About being handcuffed in front of my brothers.

About hunger so loud it talks to you.

About the wreck that shattered my body and the stillness that made me hear my own spirit.

About transition—not as a costume change, but as a coming home.

Sometimes I'll tell the story straight.

Sometimes I'll break it into lines because that's how the memory lands in my body.

Sometimes I'll slip into lessons—because the moment something happened, it started teaching me.

Read however you need to read.

Pause when it hurts.

Come back when you're ready.

Here's what I want you to know before you turn the page:

You are not what happened to you.

You are not your worst decisions.

You can be both wounded and worthy at the same time.

Becoming yourself is not selfish.

And as long as you're breathing, you are allowed to begin again.

I'm still healing.

Still growing.

Still figuring this life out in real time.

But I am not who I was.

And neither do you have to be.

Take a breath.

Turn the page.

— Tremaine

Dedication to Mama

To my mother—
for the love you offered,
the love you learned,
and the humility to apologize for the rest.
Your growth, your tears, and your truth mattered.
Thank you.
I love you.

Dedication to Mariah

To Mariah—
for the years,
the laughter,
the heartbreak,
the healing,
and the love that never left —
even when life pulled us in different directions.
You loved me back to life more times than you know.
Thank you.

Dedication to My Brothers

To my brothers—
you were my first responsibility,
my first heartbreak,
my first purpose.
I'm sorry for the hurt,
grateful for the forgiveness,
and proud of the strength we built together.
I love you all deeply.

PROLOGUE

"The Day My Life Split in Two"

There are moments in life that don't just happen —
they divide you.

Before.
And after.

For me, that moment came as a sound.

Metal folding into metal.
Bone turning to dust.
A green light shifting from "go" to "gone."
My body weightless one second
and broken the next.

December 12, 2022.

I remembered the sky.
I remembered the traffic.
I remembered thinking about dinner and getting home before rush hour.
I remembered telling myself, You'll be okay,
right before the world proved me wrong.

I didn't remember the impact.
But I remembered what came after:

Silence that didn't feel like silence.
Bright white that didn't feel like light.
Then a darkness so deep it felt like a place
I wasn't meant to return from.

I remembered voices —
shaking, urgent, afraid for me.
I remembered trying to lift my legs
and feeling nothing but fire.

I remembered the pressure on my stomach,
the frantic instructions,
the scream that didn't sound like mine.

I remembered thinking,
This is how my father died.

And wondering why I hadn't.

Five surgeries and two days later —
arms wrapped shoulder to wrist,
pelvis bolted together with metal,
catheter in place,
body half machine
and spirit half missing —
I didn't know it yet,

but the crash hadn't ended my life.

It had handed me back a different one.

One I didn't recognize.
One I wasn't ready for.
One I would have to learn to walk into
with eight rods,
twenty-six screws,
and a past I could no longer outrun.

This story isn't about the crash.
It's about the road that led to it
and the road that began after.

It's about the child who wiped a mother's tears at six.
The hunger that shaped the mind.
The violence that shaped the reflexes.
The mistakes that built the scars.
The love that saved the soul.
The addictions that chased the spirit.

The wrecks — literal and otherwise —
that tried to end the story before it could begin.

It's about the truth I spent decades avoiding:

I wasn't meant to die.
I was meant to become.

And if you're holding this book,
something in you is ready to become too.

This isn't a story about survival.

It's a story about return —
returning to the self you were forced to abandon
for safety, silence, obedience, survival, or someone else's comfort.
It's a story about truth waking up inside a broken body.
A story about the fire a person carries
even when life tries to put it out.

This isn't the beginning.

This is the moment right before the beginning —
the inhale before the first step,
the pause before the rise.

Turn the page.

Chapter 1

"The Last Day I Was a Child"

I was six years old the day my childhood ended.

I didn't know it then.
All I knew was my mother's face was wet with tears,
and my father was never coming home.

He died on a motorcycle.

One minute he was riding under an open sky—
the next, he was gone.

No warning.
No goodbye.
Just silence
and a hole in the world that nothing ever filled.

When she told me, I didn't cry.
I wiped my mother's tears with my tiny hands and whispered,
"Don't cry, Mama.
I'll take care of you."

I meant it.
Even though I had no idea what those words would cost me.

From that moment on,
I stopped being a child
and became a soldier—
a caretaker,
a shield,
a survivor.

The world didn't slow down to let me grieve.
It spun faster,
shredding everything familiar
until all that was left was hunger,
noise,
and rage.

Hunger Was Our First Language

The laughter disappeared first.
The food was next.
Home became hunger and noise and rage.

We were always hungry.
The fridge stayed empty.

I remember the pot of oatmeal I burned so badly
it turned black and bubbled like tar.
She made us eat it anyway.

Every day.
For three days.

We gagged.
We threw up.
We cried.
We starved.

Until I finally dumped it outside
before she got home.

There was one night that branded that lesson into my body.

I was about ten when my mom and her best friend decided to get a place together.
Four adults.
Five kids.
Not enough food.

By then, I already understood the unspoken rule:
Food wasn't for kids to touch freely.
You ate when grown folks said you could eat.
You didn't just "go in the kitchen."

But hunger doesn't care about rules.

One night my stomach was gnawing at me so hard I couldn't sleep.
I got up anyway.
Quiet.

Slow.
Bare feet on cold floor.

I went straight for what I loved most—
the Hawaiian bread.
Soft. Sweet.
The only thing in that house that ever tasted like comfort.

I cracked the bag open as gently as I could.
That sweetness hit my nose, and for a second, nothing else existed.

Then I heard it.

A bed creak.
Footsteps.
Someone waking up.

Panic hit me faster than hunger ever did.

I couldn't be caught in that kitchen.
Not with food in my hand.
So I did the first thing my fear told me to do:

I darted into the pantry.

I didn't realize the inside doorknob was broken.
Didn't realize the door would swing back just enough
to close flush against my stomach.

I tried to stop it.
Too late.

The edge of that door dug into my skin so hard
it carved a line across my stomach.

I remember the shock before the pain,
the way warm blood soaked into my shirt,
the way my body learned in one instant
that in this house, even trying to eat could get you cut open.

That night I paid with blood
and a scar I still carry to this day.

The next day, the lesson came with a uniform.

The cops showed up.

They didn't arrest me,
but they didn't have to.

The cold metal of the cuffs around my wrists
said everything they wanted me to hear:

Don't sneak.
Don't reach.
Don't step out of line.
Not even for bread.

Even if the arrest wasn't carried out,
the message was.

Loud.
Clear.
My mom's friend moved out but the message was permanent.

The Oldest of Four

I was the oldest.
So I became the parent.

Not because I wanted to—
but because no one else would.

I wiped my brothers' faces.
Found scraps of food when there were none.
Held their hands during storms that weren't weather.
Carried them into hiding when the house filled with yelling.

One of the places we lived had an attic—
small, dusty, cracked around the edges—
but it was ours.

I turned it into a fortress:

Blankets for walls.
An old TV that only worked half the time.
A long extension cord I managed to snake through the attic door
so we could have light
and pretend we were somewhere else.

Whenever the screaming started downstairs—
her voice or her boyfriend's—
I grabbed my brothers,
one still a toddler clinging to my shirt,
and we climbed into that little world I'd built for us.

Up there, under slanted beams and a patchwork ceiling,
we whispered stories
and laughed soft enough not to get caught.

Glass would shatter below us,
doors would slam,
fists would hit walls—or worse—
but we pretended we couldn't hear.

For a few hours,
we could breathe without fear.

The Protector Who Became a Storm

But pain has a way of leaking out sideways.

And when I didn't know where to put mine,
I put it on them.

Physically.
Emotionally.

I hated myself for it then,
and I still hate it now.

I was their protector and their abuser—
their safe place and their storm.

I was a child trying to raise children
while drowning in trauma I didn't have the language for.

They've told me they forgive me.
That they know I was young and hurting.
But I still carry the weight of it.

And I always will.

Doctor's Orders

After my father died,
the doctors gave her pills to "cope."
They didn't bring her back.
They buried her deeper.

When she wasn't sleeping like a corpse,
she was screaming.
There was no middle ground.

We dreaded the sound of her keys in the door.
We learned to move like shadows,
to breathe quietly,
to disappear in plain sight.

School became our escape—
not for education,
but for the two guaranteed hot meals.

Home was hunger,
chaos,
and the threat of violence in every room.

No man she loved ever stayed.
But every time one left,
we paid for it unintentionally.

She blamed me for everything:

Her loneliness.
Her boyfriends cheating.
Her depression.
Her exhaustion.
Her reflection in the mirror.
Her life falling apart.

"I have to love you,
but I don't like you,"
she once told me.

I believed her but, I know now she was just frustrated.

The Moves That Broke Us

We started moving right after Daddy died.
New houses.
New neighborhoods.
New schools.
New promises that this time would be different.

It never was.

By ninth grade,
I had attended over twenty schools.

Twenty times I walked into a classroom
and tried to blend into a crowd
that already knew I wouldn't be there long.

Twenty times I learned the same brutal truth:

Nothing good stays.

Eventually, I stopped bothering to learn faces.
Stopped unpacking.
Stopped hoping.

When you move that much,
hope isn't comfort—
it's a liability.

You survive.
You don't dream.

Chapter 2

"Lessons in Injustice"

By fourteen, I had already seen more than most grown men.
We were living at my grandmother's house—
another place where love was conditional
and survival was something you didn't get to negotiate.

Still… I was trying.

I had a job at a daycare,
walking distance from where we stayed.
Helping raise other people's kids
while the child still left in me fought to stay alive.

It wasn't glamorous.
But it was something.

A thread of normal life I could grip with both hands
and pretend it wouldn't snap.

One afternoon after work, I started the walk home—
tired, quiet, praying nothing would set my grandmother off
when I walked through the door.

I didn't have a phone to call my mom
to make sure she was home and I wouldn't be alone with grandma.
So when I passed a house with a yard sale out front,
I stopped and asked the woman
if I could use her phone—
just to check if my mom was there.

She looked at me like I was a threat.

"Get out of my yard," she snapped.

I stepped back, hands up,
trying to explain I meant no harm—
that I just needed to make a quick call.

She didn't care.
She picked up a bat
and threw it at me.

Not swung.
Not threatened.
Threw it.

Then she came toward me.

I panicked.
Grabbed the bat
and ran.

Not to fight.
Not to steal.
Just to get away alive.

A few houses down, I dropped it
and kept walking.
Heart pounding.
Trying to breathe.
Trying to make it home.

That's when a police car passed.
Slowed.
Reversed.
Stopped.

The door flew open.

"Hands on the hood."

I froze.

"Why?" I asked.
"I haven't done anything—"

He didn't answer.
Just slammed me onto the hood.
Metal against my cheek.
Pain everywhere.

I turned my head to ask again—
just to understand—
and that's when he pulled out his baton.

He didn't wait.
Didn't warn me.

He just started swinging.

Back.
Arms.
Ribs.
Shoulders.

Another officer got out.
Joined in.
No hesitation.
No questions.
No humanity.

Just violence.

They threw me in the back of the car like trash—
a problem handled.

Then finally, after the beating,
after the cuffs,
after the humiliation,
they asked my name.

"Latreece," I said.
"I'm fourteen."

I will never forget the look they exchanged.
Shock.
Guilt.
Fear.
Recognition.

Maybe they thought I was older.
Maybe the clothes confused them.
I hadn't transitioned yet—
just a young girl in boys' clothes,
trying to exist.

They drove me to my grandmother's house.
Dropped me off.
Said nothing.

I told her everything—
every hit,
every bruise,

every detail of how they attacked me
before asking a single question.

She didn't believe me.

They said I was lying.

Of course they did.

No report.
No apology.
No accountability.

Just another wound erased from paperwork
but carved forever into memory.

When my mom got home,
I showed her the bruises.
The marks.
The cuts.
The way my body shook
when I tried to replay what happened.

She believed me.

But belief didn't fix anything.

The police denied it all.
No record of the stop.
No record of the assault.
Just two men with badges
and a kid they decided didn't matter.

Guess who the world believed.

That day, I learned something permanent—
something carved into me deeper than any bruise:

Justice wasn't built for kids like me.

It wasn't built for brown skin.
It wasn't built for broken homes.
It wasn't built for children who survived chaos.
It wasn't built for anyone
without money, protection,
or a last name with weight.

Justice was built for people
who didn't look like me,
didn't live like me,
didn't hurt like me.

After that,
I stopped asking the system for fairness.
Stopped expecting anyone to save me.
Stopped believing truth was enough.

Somewhere deep inside,
even at fourteen,
I knew:

If I was going to survive this life,
I couldn't play by their rules.
I'd have to make my own.

Chapter 3

"The Truth I Carried to Jacksonville"

But before Jacksonville,
before the band room and MySpace and first love,
before any of the choices people judged me for—
there was a wound I carried alone.

A wound I didn't create.
A wound I didn't ask for.
A wound that shaped everything that came after.

The truth is…
I was touched.

Not by a stranger.
Not by a monster hiding in an alley.

By the man my mother trusted enough to share a home with.

He tried it once —
breath sour with Black & Milds and liquor,
voice low with excuses meant to sound like affection.

He caressed me,
told me he was the only one who should touch me like that,
and then he laid on top of me
and stuck his tongue in my mouth.

I pushed him off.

He wasn't expecting strength from a kid.
But survival grows muscles you can't see.

He stumbled, straightened up,
looked at me with drunken certainty and said:

"A drunk heart speaks a sober mind.
Don't tell nobody."

Then he left my room
like he had just borrowed something instead of breaking something.

I held that secret longer than any child should.
Held it until it nearly rotted me from the inside out.

And when I finally told my mother —
when I gathered every ounce of courage in my small, shaking body —
she didn't put him out.

She didn't protect me.

She let him stay.

That moment cut deeper than anything he did to me physically.
Because betrayal from a stranger wounds you.
But betrayal from a parent rearranges your soul.

At the time, all I understood was:
I wasn't worth saving.

But years later —
after time, distance, healing, and hard conversations —
my mother told me the truth behind her choice.

We talked about it a few years ago.
Really talked.

She said she was torn.
Said she was young.
Broken.
Grieving.
Alone.
And afraid.

She told me she believed if she put him out,
we would've been homeless with four kids.
No food.
No money.
No safety net.
No plan.

She said she chose what she thought would keep us sheltered —
even if it meant sacrificing my safety.

Then she looked at me and said words I never expected:

"If I could go back...
I would have put him out.
I would have taken the homelessness.
Because the damage to you —
and to us —
was worse than anything poverty could've done."

Her honesty didn't erase what happened.
Didn't patch the hole.
Didn't unwrite the memory.

But it did something important:

It returned the responsibility
to the adult who should've carried it all along.

And it helped me release a shame
that was never mine to hold.

Everything that came after —
the anger,
the rebellion,
the skipping school,
the stealing,
the running,
the numbness I mistook for strength —
it didn't grow out of nowhere.

It grew from silence.
From betrayal.
From the moment a child learned
that protection wasn't guaranteed,
and sometimes the people you love
choose survival over your innocence.

That was the truth I carried into Jacksonville.

That was the version of me who arrived in "Jack and Kill."

That was the kid who walked into a church and met Mariah.

A kid already cracked open,
already searching for safety,
already trying to become whole in a world that kept trying to break them.

And now, you know the truth of what I survived
before the next chapter began.

Chapter 4

"Jack and Kill & Holy Ground"

When my mother told us we were moving to Jacksonville, Florida,
she said it was one of the top ten places in the country to raise a family.

She was wrong.

The year we moved there, Jacksonville was the murder capital.
Locals didn't call it Jacksonville—they called it Jack and Kill.

But the neighborhood we ended up in was quiet.
Not good.
Not safe.
Just... quiet.

The kind of quiet that feels like holding your breath.
Where people kept to themselves.
Windows stayed closed even on sunny days.
You learned fast not to expect smiles from strangers.

I started high school at Robert E. Lee—
a public school graded F by the state,
named after a man who fought to keep people like me enslaved.

It fit.

Even there, in a place forgotten by the system,
something small and stubborn inside me reached for hope.

I joined the band.

I played baritone.
The uniforms were worn and faded.
The instruments were held together with duct tape and prayer.
But music gave me a reason to breathe.

That's where I met Gert—
a tuba player—
and his best friend, BooBoo.

We clicked fast.
The three of us became our own little family
in a place that didn't have much use for the word.

They made me laugh when all I wanted to do was disappear.

The Blame Game

My mom blamed me for every man who left,
for every unpaid bill,
for every problem in her life.

But the night she beat me bloody
is one I still remember with perfect clarity.

It began like most nights—
with shouting.

Her face twisted in a rage
that had nothing to do with me
and everything to do with what life had done to her.

She slapped me first.
Then her fists came next.
Over and over.

My nose burst.
Blood soaked my shirt.

I didn't fight back.
Didn't raise a hand.
Didn't run.

Part of me still believed
if I stayed still enough,
obedient enough,
quiet enough—
she would stop.

She didn't.

When it was over,
she picked up the phone.

Not to help me.
Not to apologize.

She called the police.

When they arrived,
she told them I attacked her.

I showed them the dried blood on my shirt,
still warm on my skin.

They didn't care.

They saw what they wanted:

A "problem child."
Not a wounded kid.

They handcuffed me right there in the living room
while my brothers watched—
too terrified to move.

On the ride to the station,
I didn't cry.
Didn't beg.

I knew better.

In my world,
truth never stood a chance.

All that mattered
was getting rid of me.

And that's exactly what they did.

First High

When I got back I was worse off then before. One afternoon back at Lee, Gert, BooBoo, and I skipped class for the first time. Walked off campus and headed to a park nearby.

It felt reckless.
Wrong.
Free.

At the park, Gert pulled out a joint and asked if I smoked.

I lied.
Said yes.
Because I needed to belong
more than I needed to tell the truth.

I took my first hit at fourteen.
The world softened around the edges.
The weight on my chest lifted, just a little.

For a moment, I wasn't the problem child,
the broken one,
the kid with the past.

I was just there.

Alive.
Laughing.
Free.

It didn't stay innocent for long.

Mariah

I met her at church.

Of all places.

My mother had gotten wrapped up in a church we found after moving
to Jacksonville—
the same church where her boyfriend,
the man who had hurt me,
was still welcomed like family.

The same church that was supposed to "fix" me.

I didn't expect anything good to come from there.
I didn't expect her.

Mariah.

The first time I saw her, something shifted in me.
I didn't have language for it.
Didn't have theology for it.
Didn't have safety for it.

All I knew was she made me nervous
in a way that felt more like hope than fear.

Every Tuesday, Wednesday, and Sunday, I found a reason to be near her.
I even joined choir just to see her on Thursdays, too.

Gert would let me borrow his phone after school
so I could talk to her all day.

At night, I would sneak into my mother's office,
lock the door,
and log onto MySpace.

Mariah was my world inside that screen.
My peace.
My proof that somehow, after everything,
I was still capable of being loved.

We messaged for hours—
our words glowing in the dark.
She was my background picture.
I was hers.
We wrote vows in our profiles,
teenage promises loud and reckless and real.

We kissed for the first time in the dark of the church bathroom.
The pastor's daughter was inside to make it less suspicious
that we were in there together.

We were terrified of being caught,
terrified someone would break what we'd found.

We didn't want to hurt anyone.

But for once,
we had something that made sense in a world that never had.

Mariah was my peace in a war I didn't know how to win.
She was the first person who made me feel
like I wasn't broken beyond repair.

She was home.

Chapter 5

"The Door"

It all started with a door.

I was in my mother's office—
the only place in that house
where I could breathe without waiting for the next explosion.

Every night, after the screaming died down,
after my brothers fell asleep,
after my mother passed out or left with whatever man was around that week,
I would sneak into that office.

Close the door.
Lock it.
Exhale.

Then I'd log in.

Mariah was waiting on the other side of the screen.
Her words were a lifeline.
Her presence was proof I hadn't imagined the good in me.

We talked for hours.
We were in love.
We weren't sorry.

MySpace still glowed on the monitor when it happened.

The banging.

My heart slammed into my ribs.

I fumbled,
closed the tab,
unlocked the door.

Too late.

My mother shoved past me,
went straight for the computer,
pulled up the history,
clicked the last page.

There we were.

Mariah's face.
Our vows.
Our love—wide open,
no longer ours.

The panic wasn't about being "caught."
It was about what I knew would come next.

I didn't feel guilty for loving Mariah.
I felt guilty because I knew what her mother would do.
Knew Mariah would pay for something
that had felt like the first safe thing in my life.

I begged my mother.

"Please don't call.
Don't tell her mom.
Please... she'll hurt her."

It didn't matter.

The phone was already in her hand.

Holy Ground, Dirty Hands

That night, they dragged us both to the church.

The place that claimed it was built on love.
The place that turned its back
the moment love didn't look the way they wanted it to.

The pastor was there.
The First Lady.
My mother.
Mariah's mother.
And my mother's boyfriend—

the same man who had laid his hands on me,
the same man they all knew about,
the same man still welcomed in God's house
while we were the ones on trial.

They sat us in the front pews,
under cheap sanctuary lights,
under their judgment,
under the weight of their disgust.

They told us to delete everything.

Our pages.
Our pictures.
Our words.
Our love.

They asked if we thought what we did was right.

I couldn't speak.

Fear smothered my voice.

Mariah answered for both of us.

"It might be wrong, but it feels right, we're in love" she said.

Her voice was soft,
but steady.

Her mother hit her.
Right there.
In front of everyone.

The pastor stepped in, tried to calm her down,
but the damage was done.

Mariah begged not to go home.

Begged the pastor.
Begged the First Lady.

"Please don't send me with her," she said.

They did anyway.

They always do.

We were told never to speak again.
Never to look for each other.
Never to hold on to anything we had built.

When Mariah turned away from me that night,
I didn't see anger.

I saw heartbreak.

She wasn't scared of the punishment.
She was scared of losing me.

And there was nothing I could do.

The First Loss

After that, Mariah disappeared.

Her mother moved her to another church.
No more choir.
No more stolen glances.
No more late-night IMs.

Just silence,
where her laughter used to echo.

I tried to swallow it.
Tried to act like it was just another loss
on a long list of losses.

It wasn't.

Mariah wasn't just a person to me.
She was the last piece of childhood I was still holding on to.

The last reason I believed
there was something good left in me.

When they took her,
something in me broke for good.

It would be months before she found her way back to me.
Months before a Facebook message lit my world up again.

But by then,
I was already falling.

Chapter 6

"Falling, Failing, Finishing Anyway"

After they tore Mariah away from me,
I didn't explode.

I eroded.

Piece by piece.
Day by day.

Until the version of me that laughed,
that dreamed,
that hoped—
was just smoke.

I still got up every morning.
Still caught the school bus.
Still walked the halls of Robert E. Lee High
like I had somewhere to be.

But I wasn't there.

Skipping Reality

I skipped class so often
it stopped feeling like rebellion.

It felt like breathing.

I'd meet Gert and BooBoo off campus—
same parks,
same streets,
same broken sidewalks.

We smoked until the world blurred
and my chest didn't feel so tight.
Passed around cheap liquor in soda bottles.
Laughed too loud at nothing
because laughing at something real
might make us crumble.

Sometimes I wondered if anyone at school could tell.
If they saw it in my face—

how my smile never fully reached my eyes,
how my jokes were always half a beat behind my pain.

Maybe they didn't.
Maybe I even fooled myself
for a few hours a day.

Because as soon as the last bell rang,
reality came crashing back.

I had to be home when school ended.

To watch my brothers.
To cook.
To clean.
To be a second parent and a broken child at the same time.

All my dirt happened in the daylight.
All my sadness came at night.

I cried myself to sleep more nights than I can count.
Begged God to let me be eighteen already—
like a number would magically unlock freedom.

Stealing to Stay Alive

I didn't start stealing with Blue.

I started in elementary.

Snacks from classmates' desks.
Coins from the lost-and-found.
A few bills from a teacher's purse when she wasn't looking.

It wasn't greed.
It was survival.

Hunger.
Habit.
Desperation.

When the world gives you nothing,
you learn how to take what you need
to stay standing.

By the time I met Blue,
stealing wasn't new.

I knew how to read a room.
Who looked vulnerable.
Who wouldn't fight back.
What I could get away with.

So when I told Blue about the kid with the laptop,
it wasn't a spur-of-the-moment thing.

It was a plan.

I picked the target.
Picked the time.
Explained what we were going to do.

It happened in the outdoor cafeteria,
right on campus,
middle of the day.

Blue grabbed the laptop and ran,
just like we said he would.

I walked away like I had nothing to do with it.

But I did.

Every bit of it was mine.

When the school caught on,
Blue folded fast.

He said it was all me.
Said he had nothing to do with it.

And I didn't name him.

Not because I was loyal—
but because I was tired.

Because part of me believed I deserved it.
That this was who I was now:

A thief.
A liar.
A threat.

I had built my own fall
and now it was time to hit the ground.

Mr. Whitehead

They called me to the office like it was any other day.
No sirens.
No yelling.
Just my name over the intercom.

I knew why.
I didn't panic.
Didn't run.
Didn't lie.

When I walked in,
Mr. Whitehead, the dean, was waiting.

Old white man.
Hard face.
Soft eyes.

He had seen me move from skipping grades
to sitting in AP classes.
He knew I was smart.
Knew I was capable.
Knew I didn't belong where I was heading.

When I sat down,
he was crying.

He didn't shout.
Didn't throw words like "failure" or "criminal" at me.

He just shook his head,
eyes full of grief that wasn't just for me—
it was for every kid like me
he had watched the system chew up.

He told me I was throwing my life away.
Told me he believed in me.
Meant it.

And then he expelled me.

Because even when someone cares,
the machine they work for
doesn't.

I didn't cry.
Didn't beg.

I just nodded
and walked out.

A door closed behind me.

But if I'm honest,
that door had been closing for a long time.

This was just the last sound it made.

Back to Texas

After the robbery,
after the expulsion,
after Mr. Whitehead cried for me and cut me loose—

my mom decided we were moving again.

This time back to Texas.
Back to where it all started.
Back to old ghosts and unfinished business.

She called it a fresh start.
Said I'd have better chances.
Said nobody needed to know what happened in Florida.

But she wasn't saving me.

She was saving herself.

She didn't want her child to be
"the kid who caught a felony in Jacksonville."
Didn't want the story following us
through family conversations and holiday tables.

So we packed.
We left.
No therapy.
No apology.
No closure.

Just boxes.
Silence.
And me, carrying the weight.

I enrolled at Westfield High a few weeks after we got back.

Tried to keep my head down.

But you can't outrun a story you've already swallowed.

I got pulled from class.
No warning.
No explanation I could understand.

"Alternative placement: High Point."

High Point wasn't school.
It was storage.

A warehouse for kids no one wanted to deal with.
A room full of trauma in hoodies and headphones.

Desks full of stories like mine—
unheard, unmanaged, mislabeled.

They said it was temporary.

Eventually, they sent me back to Westfield.
But I was already gone.

I skipped more than I stayed.
Some days I didn't go at all.

Then the letters started.

Truancy notices.
Legal threats.

Not against me—
against my mother.

If I didn't show up,
she would be held responsible.

So she made a choice.

She didn't ask how I was doing.
Didn't ask why I couldn't stand being there.
Didn't ask what I needed.

She made me drop out.

Not because I didn't deserve an education.
Because she didn't want to go to jail.

And honestly?
I understand.

But understanding doesn't make it hurt less.

My Mother, As I Know Her Now

People may try to say my mom never tried.
That she didn't care.
That she was just absent.

It's not that simple.

She did talk.
She did try—
in her own way.

But the moment my feelings pointed back at her,
she shut down.

If I said I was hurt,
I was "ungrateful."

If I said I was angry,
she said I'd infected my brothers with it—
that their rage came from me.

But where did mine come from?

I know the answer.
She does too.

She lost her husband at twenty-three.
Became a widow with two kids.

Had her world ripped apart
It took 20 years to put it back together.

I watched her grieve.
I watched pills replace sleep.
I watched men replace stability.

I saw her pain.

I just wish she could've seen mine at the time.

Mariah Finds Me Again

I don't believe in coincidence—
not with Mariah.

By the time she came back into my life,
I had dropped out of high school.
Been labeled "too much" and "too far gone."
I was nowhere,
going nowhere,
surrounded by noise and swallowed by silence.

My sister—my dad's daughter,
but always just my sister—
got a message on Facebook one day.

"Do you know Tee Criner?"

Our last name isn't common.
It stood out.

It was Mariah.

When my sister called and told me,
my whole body lit up.

I didn't think.
I just called.

She answered.

Her voice sounded the same—
like no time had passed,
like the world hadn't tried to tear us apart.

We slipped right back into us.

No awkward catch-up.
No distance to bridge.
Just two hearts that knew their way back.

Getting her back felt like coming home—
not to the place I was from,
but to the place I had been surviving for.

Finishing Anyway

By the time I enrolled in homeschool,
I didn't believe I'd finish.

I had dropped out.
Been expelled.
Been labeled and sorted and set aside.

But I was still breathing.
Still trying.

Mariah was there the whole time.

We were still long distance.
Still in separate worlds,
bonded by late-night calls and stubborn love.

She never made me feel like I was too far gone.
Never held my past over my head.

She just kept saying she was proud of me.

"I'm proud of you for finishing your classes,"
she told me one night.

I didn't tell her right away
that I had passed everything—
except one thing:

The essay.

The topic didn't feel real.
I couldn't latch onto it.
Every time I tried to write,
my brain froze.

I was embarrassed.
After everything I'd survived,
this was what I was stuck on?

When I finally told her,
she didn't laugh.
Didn't judge.

"I'll help," she said.

And she meant it.

She wrote it.
Clean.
Effortless.
Brilliant.

I passed with flying colors.

There was no cap-and-gown ceremony.
No name echoing in a gym.
No stadium applause.

But my mother did take me to Walmart for graduation pictures.
She bought me a cap and gown—
not borrowed,
not patched together,
bought.

She let me dress how I wanted.
Let me wear her black stud diamond earrings.

After years of trying to pray my "spirit of homosexuality" away,
years of calling my identity a problem,
she let me show up in those photos
as myself.

I still don't know if she was proud of me
or proud of the picture she could show other people.

But for once,
that wasn't the important part.

Because I knew the truth:

I had finished something
the world never thought I could.

And I hadn't done it alone.

Mariah had been with me the whole way—
the same girl they dragged away from me in a church pew—

now helping me quietly finish
what they never believed I'd start.

Chapter 7

"Willie, the Run, and the First Escape"

I met Willie at the bus stop.

Before the dropout.
Before the felonies.
Back when I still showed up to school,
even if my mind never made it past the front doors.

He was wild from the jump.
Goofy, sharp, a little reckless—
the kind of kid who laughed too loud
and made trouble feel like an invitation instead of a warning.

We clicked instantly.

Two kids with different stories,
same ache underneath:

No safety.
No structure.
No one really looking out for us in any consistent way.

He lived a few doors down.

Not in the projects.
Not in an apartment complex.
Just a house on a street that looked "normal"
if you were only driving through.

But we lived there.

We knew the truth.

There weren't gunshots at night,
but there was heat in the daylight.
Kids like us got paid by drug dealers to act as lookouts—
to whistle when we saw police cars swing the corner.

We learned quick:

What to say.
What not to say.
Who to trust.
Who to avoid.
How to keep our heads down
while watching everything.

It wasn't war-zone energy.
It was hustle energy.
Survival energy.

And we picked it up fast.

When my mom left for work during the day,
I slipped out the house.

Me and Willie ran the neighborhood like ghosts.
Smoked until everything felt far away.
Walked until the silence in our chests didn't feel so heavy anymore.

At night, we broke into cars.

Sliding through driveways and cul-de-sacs like shadows.
Checking doors.
Looking under seats.
Snatching loose change, chargers, laptops, money, weapons—
anything we could take, sell, trade, or flip into distraction.

We weren't thrill-seekers.

We were survivors.

We weren't evil.
We were hungry.
Tired.
Bored.
Ignored.

What started as a joke
became routine.

Slide the door.
Check the console.
Hit the next one.

We were always high.
Always moving.

I didn't realize how deep we were in.
Not at first.

I just knew that with Willie,
the world didn't feel as sharp.

He didn't ask me to be anything.
Didn't judge my moods, my triggers, my silence.
He just existed beside me.

He became my brother.
No blood required.

Sometimes I think that friendship saved my life.
Other times I think it nearly ended it.

The truth is,
it did both.

And he's still here.

After everything—
he's still here.

People like that don't come around twice.

Flags on the Top Shelf

She found them one afternoon.

I don't know what she was looking for.
Maybe she was snooping.
Maybe she just needed a reason.

Either way, she opened my closet, looked up—
and saw them.

The flags.

Folded bandanas.
Red and black.
Stacked neatly on the top shelf
like trophies or targets.

She dragged them down,
stormed into the room,
and threw them on the floor in front of me
like they were weapons.

"What is this?" she snapped.

Not curious.
Not concerned.

Already angry.
Already disgusted.
Already building her narrative.

I didn't answer.

What could I say?

That I had joined a gang?
That codes and colors felt safer than our living room?
That being claimed by something—
even something dangerous—
felt more secure
than never being claimed by her?

That I needed someone to protect me
because she never did?

She kept yelling.
Accusing.
Pacing.
Spitting rage in my direction.

Her voice faded into background noise.

All I could hear was the pounding in my own chest.

My fists clenched.
Jaw locked.

Something swelled inside me—
bigger than rage,
heavier than hate.

I wasn't going to hit her.
I didn't want to.

But tightening every muscle in my body
gave me somewhere to put the scream
I couldn't let out.

"You just don't know…"
I started.

The rest got stuck.

But inside, the words were loud:

You don't know how much you hurt me.
How many nights I cried.
How many times I needed you
and you were sleeping, screaming, or gone.
You don't know.

And you never tried to.

I wanted to say it all.
To scream it so loud
it broke through every wall she'd built between us.

But I didn't.

All she saw
were my fists.

To this day, she still tells people,
"I saw what she could do to me that day."

Like I was a threat.
Like I stood over her with violence in my eyes.

But she didn't see violence.

She saw truth trying to break through.
A child on the edge—
not of rage,
but of collapse.

I wasn't about to hurt her.

I was finally about to be honest.

And she never let me.

Not then.
Not ever.

Two Felonies and a Mother's Decision

I just wanted to get out.

That's all it was.

Not to be reckless.
Not to hurt anyone.

I just needed to feel free.

So I took the truck.

My mom's.
Middle of the night.
No plan.
No destination.

I just drove.

Windows down.
Air hitting my face like a kind of baptism.
Like maybe, finally,
I could breathe.

I ended up in Conroe.
Don't even remember how.

Just roads and quiet and the illusion of escape.

I was sixteen.
No license.
No idea how fast things could go wrong.

He pulled me over for a blinker.

A blinker.

Routine stop.
Flashlight.
Questions.

License and registration.

"I don't have a license," I said.
"It's my mom's truck."

"Does she know you have it?"

"No."

He asked for her number.
I gave it to him.

He called.

She answered.

And without a pause,
without a single question for me,
without asking if I was okay,
she said:

"I want to press charges."

That hit harder than the arrest.
Harder than the cuffs.
Harder than the backseat cage of the squad car.

That was the moment I knew:

She was never going to save me.
Not now.
Not ever.

They charged me with two first-degree felonies:

Theft over $1,500.
Unlawful Use of a Motor Vehicle.

Didn't matter that it was my mother's truck.
Didn't matter that I wasn't joyriding with a crew,
just a kid trying to feel air in his lungs.

What mattered was that I was sixteen,
Black,
and disposable.

And the one person who could've stopped it
chose not to.

She made me a criminal that night.

The system just followed her lead.

They took me.
Processed me.
Labeled me.

Felon.
At sixteen.

Gone.
Again.

House Arrest and Screwed Windows

Coming home wasn't a return.
It was a sentence.

The charges didn't land as hard as they could have—
but the punishment still did.

House arrest.

An ankle monitor.
No school.
No friends.
No freedom.

The only place I was allowed to go
was work.

My mom got me a daycare job
through one of her trainings.

I wasn't passionate about kids.
I was passionate about air.

About leaving the house.
About not rotting in a living room with boarded freedom.

She took every paycheck.

Every dollar.

I worked.
She spent.

I remember one check in particular.
She didn't even let it touch my hands.
She walked it straight to the church—
some carnival fundraiser.

Didn't ask.
Didn't thank me.

Just tithed my labor
without my consent.

The house became a cage.

She had the windows screwed shut—
drilled in, permanent.
Deadbolted the front and back doors from the inside
and took the keys with her.

If I wasn't at the daycare,
I was locked in.

She called it protection, she was worried.

At the time, I felt it was possession.

I cried quietly at night.
Not just over what had happened,
but what never got the chance to.

There was no future here.
No version of me that got to grow.

I was surviving.
Barely.

Then came Key.

Key and the First Escape

She was older.
Twenty-six.
Three kids.
A different kind of wild.

I don't remember how we started talking.
Maybe in passing.
Maybe because I looked like a storm waiting to happen.

She asked questions.
Listened.

I told her about my mom.
The locked windows.
The stolen checks.
The deadbolted doors.

She wasn't shocked.
She was… interested.

One day, she handed me a cellphone.

"Use it when you need to talk," she said.
"When you need a break."

It was the first thing in a long time
that felt like a gift.

No strings.
Or so I thought.

Eventually, she offered more:

"If you can get the house key,
I'll make a copy."

That way, when my mom locked me in at night,
I could slip out.
Walk down the steps.
Meet her nearby.

Sometimes we just sat and talked.
Other times, we smoked.

We stayed close enough to the apartment
that my ankle monitor didn't trigger.

She introduced me to a kind of freedom
I'd only seen in movies.

Late-night drives.
Music turned up.
Windows cracked.
Real laughter.

For the first time in forever,
I felt like I was living,
not just waiting to be punished.

But I knew it couldn't last.

Nothing ever did.

The Last Run Before the Fall

The Thursday before my probation ended,
they called me in.

Removed the ankle monitor early.

"Technically, you're still under supervision until Saturday,"
they said.
"Don't mess it up."

I nodded.
Didn't say much.

Then I called Key.

That night, she picked me up.

I left.
No monitor.
No cuffs.
No track.

We spent the night together.
No fear.
Just air.

Until morning.

Her kids needed to get to school.
My mom was no doubt doing the same.

Which meant she knew I was gone.

We rushed back to the complex.
My mother was already circling the parking lot
like a shark that smelled blood.

Key eased the car around the corner.
I slid down in my seat.

The moment was tight,
the kind of pressure you can feel in your teeth.

She dropped me off a building away.
I snuck inside.

But it was already over.

My mom was on the phone with my probation officer.

When she handed me the phone,
I knew what was coming.

He said they were sending a car.

Said I'd violated.
Said I'd be taken in.

She locked the front door.
But I had a key copy now.

She told my brother to watch me
while she got the other boys ready.

I told him I was going to feed the dog.
He followed me downstairs.

But the moment my foot hit the last step—
I ran.

Unlocked the door.
Threw it open.
Jumped from the second-story porch.

Landed hard.
Kept running.

I didn't look back.

Just ran
until my lungs burned
and my legs screamed.

Anywhere but home.
Anywhere but back in a cell.

I ducked into a Popeyes a few blocks away.
Slipped inside, heart still sprinting.

No one looked twice.
Just another teenager sweating in a too-warm hoodie.

I claimed a corner booth near the bathroom,
back to the wall,
eyes on the door.

Hands shaking,
I pulled out the phone.

Called Key.

"I'm at Popeyes," I said.

She didn't ask why.

"Stay there," she said.
"I'm coming."

So I did.

Sat there, hiding in the smell of fried chicken and bleach,
waiting to disappear.

She pulled up twenty minutes later.
Silver car.
Tinted windows.

I got in.

Didn't cry.
Didn't talk.

Just… surrendered.

She didn't need the story.
She already knew the pattern.

The locked house.
The ankle monitor.
The suffocating rules.

She knew enough.

I moved in that night.

It wasn't love.
Wasn't even comfort.

It was space.

Space to breathe.
To feel.
To fall apart without an audience.

She gave me a room.
A bed.
Clothes.
Jokes that didn't end in threats.

And then she gave me access to her world
—one I wasn't ready for
but walked into anyway.

I was sixteen.
She was twenty-six.
Three kids.
Life moving fast.

We smoked.
We drank.
We hit clubs.
I swallowed party pills without asking names.

They gave me silence in my mind.

Silence,
to me,
felt like mercy.

I shaved my head.
Changed my clothes.
Changed my name.

Learned how to disappear in plain sight.
How to listen for the sound of patrol cars
before you even see the lights.

She hid me in the attic when cops drove too slow.
The fiberglass made my skin itch for hours.
Didn't matter.

It was better than cuffs.
Better than that house.
Better than going back into a system
that never wanted me whole.

Every part of my life became about not getting caught.

So I stopped taking Mariah's calls.
Stopped texting.
Stopped everything.

Not because I stopped loving her.

Because I loved her enough
not to drag her into this.

Meanwhile, I missed my brothers
like a phantom limb.

Not just their noise.
Their needing me.

So one day, I asked Key to drive me
to my youngest brother's school.

We waited by the fence.

Hood up.
Head low.
Heart punching through my chest.

I asked a kid to go find him.

He did.

The moment my brother saw me—
even with my shaved head,
even with weight dropped from my frame—
he ran to the fence.

"I missed you," he said.

I held his hands through the metal.
Cracked right there.

"I love you so much," I told him.

He smiled.
Didn't ask where I'd been.
Kids just know.

A teacher came over.
Said I had to come sign in if I wanted to visit.

But I was on the run.

So I ran.
Again.

Eventually, even Key started to crack under the weight.
She had kids of her own.
Fear of her own.

Hiding me became too much.

She started locking the door when patrol cars rolled by.
Told her kids not to say my name when guests visited.

It wasn't hate.
It was exhaustion.

We were both tired.

One night, she sat me down.

"You can't live like this," she said.

And she was right.

So I made the call.

I called my mother.

Months had passed.

She sounded shocked to hear my voice.
We met.
Talked.
Didn't yell.

I told her where I was.
What I was ready to do.

She agreed to set up a meeting with my probation officer.

I turned myself in.

They processed me.
Again.
Same story.
New timestamp.

Stamped my file: *Unsuccessful Discharge.*

Didn't matter that I came back on my own.
Didn't matter that I ran toward accountability this time.

They saw the record.
Not the effort.

And I was done.

So I went home.

Again.

By then, they were in Dallas.

New city.
Same dynamic.

She didn't hug me.
Didn't ask what I needed.

Just folded me back into the house
like another piece of furniture.

And I folded too.

Back into the role.
Back into the silence.

But I was seventeen now.

And in Texas,
that meant something.

Chapter 8

"Emancipation, One Last Attempt at Forever"

In Texas, seventeen is a threshold.

It's the line between "child" and "you're on your own."

To me, it meant this:

I could finally be emancipated since I'd graduated.

To my mother,
it meant something else:

She could finally be rid of me.

She didn't see emancipation as me stepping into adulthood.
She saw it as her chance to legally unload
what she'd been calling a burden for years.

So she did what she'd always wanted to do.

She booked a plane ticket.

To Jacksonville.
To Mariah.
To the one place my heart had been orbiting for years.

This time, I believed it.

This time, it was our turn.

Me and Mariah, together—
no hiding, no MySpace, no locked church doors.

Just us.

She still lived with her mother,
but her cousin was on our side.
We had a plan.

When that plane landed
and I saw her again—
felt her presence in real air,
not over a phone or screen—

the world stopped spinning long enough
for me to believe in forever.

We were finally in the same place,
on the same side,
with nobody sneaking up behind us
with a Bible and judgment.

At least, that's what it felt like
for a few hours.

The Knock

Forever lasted less than a day.

That night, the police showed up.

No gentle knock.
No "Can we talk?"
No questions.

Just presence.
Authority.
Hands already on their belts.

They didn't care about details.
Didn't ask who I was,
what we'd endured,
what this moment meant.

They came with an ultimatum.

One of them reached into his own pocket,
pulled out a small bag of something,
and held it up.

"If she doesn't leave with her mom," he said,
"you're getting charged with this."

They were willing to frame me
just to rip us apart.

I stared at him.
Didn't flinch.
Didn't plead.

Then he grabbed me.
Beat me.
Threw me against the car.
Forced me inside the back seat.

As I sat there—
bruised, breathless, humiliated—

I watched Mariah's mom drive her away.

Again.

They didn't care who I was.
Didn't care what we'd survived.
Didn't care that this was the second time in my life
they were ripping my heart out in front of me.

They just wanted me gone.

And they got what they came for.

Refusal to Leave

But I didn't go back.

Not right away.

They could force me into a squad car.
They couldn't force me to give up.

I refused to leave without her.

For days, I slept in the backyard
of an old classmate.

No mattress.
No blanket.
Just ground, sky, and stubborn hope.

I was willing to be homeless
before I was willing to abandon her.

I told myself I'd wait
until the universe intervened,
until something broke open,
until some path appeared.

Eventually, my mother found out where I was.

And this time,
she was the one who bought the return ticket.

Not because she missed me.
Not because she was worried for my safety.
Not because she had a change of heart.

Because she was embarrassed.

Because I had slipped out of her control—
again—
and she couldn't stand the thought
of me wandering across state lines like a stray.

She sent one of her friends to pick me up,
like I was a misdelivered package
waiting on the wrong porch.

I got in the car.

Not because I was ready.
Not because I believed going back would fix anything.

But because I was done.

Not angry.
Not even heartbroken.

Just empty.

So, so tired.

I was numb to everything except the craving.
I was drowning inside my own skin,
and the only thing that felt like air
was poison.

But life doesn't let you self-destruct forever.
Eventually, it demands payment.

And mine came on a random day
on the highway between Houston and Orange.

It was my brother's birthday weekend.
I was on my way to pick him up
and take him out.
Do something.
Anything.

Try to be the big brother I was never allowed to be
because I was always too busy surviving.

I was driving a Dodge Charger
with chrome 22s and dark tint.
Young.
Black.
Dreads.
Gold grill.

I looked exactly like the reason
cops flip their lights on without thinking.

And to make it worse —
I had spent all day tearing apart my car
because I had lost a baggie.

My mind was itching.
My body was screaming.
My thoughts were spinning so fast
they didn't sound like thoughts anymore.

Just noise.

A craving so loud
it drowned out everything else.

I didn't even notice the taillights weren't working.

I didn't notice the line of police cars on the side of the road
responding to a scene.

What I did notice
was the moment one of them peeled off,
cut across the lanes,
and flew up behind me
with lights blazing.

My stomach didn't drop.

It had already dropped months ago
when I started losing myself.

He walked up slow.
Circling my car.
Hand on his weapon.

"License and registration."

I didn't have a license.
Told him the truth.

He told me to step out of the vehicle.
I did.

Calm.

Too calm.

Addiction can turn fear into silence
and silence into surrender.

He searched the car.

And right there —
in the place I'd been tearing apart all morning —
he found the baggie.

Not even full.
But enough.

Enough to ruin everything.

Enough to turn ten years probation
into a prison sentence.

Enough to turn a broken man
into an inmate.

He cuffed me.
Shoved me into the back of the patrol car.
No words.
No sympathy.

Just another "got one" expression
on a face I didn't feel like deciphering.

Sitting there,
hands bound,
future dissolving—

all I could think was:

"How did I get here again?"

Not the legal answer.
Not the psychological one.

The real one.

I got here
because I was tired,
and lost,
and addicted,
and hurting,
and pretending to be okay,
and trying to outrun pain that had a ten-year head start on me.

I got here
because nobody taught me how to cope.
Only how to survive.

When I finally went to court,
after months of sitting in jail,
they gave me a choice:

**Six months inpatient rehab
OR
five years in prison.**

At first I lost it.

I wasn't an addict.
That's what I told myself.

I wasn't like the others.
That's what I lied to myself.

But sitting in that cell,
running it through my mind over and over,
I finally asked the question
I'd spent my whole life avoiding:

"If you're not an addict,
why choose prison over help?"

The answer hit me hard:

Because prison felt familiar.
Because pain felt normal.
Because healing felt impossible.

And that scared me more than incarceration.

So I pushed the call button and said:

"I need help."

Not proudly.
Not bravely.
Not poetically.

Just truthfully.

Because for the first time in my life,
I understood:

**If I didn't choose life,
I was choosing death.**

And that simple decision —
that one crack in my denial —
led to the place where I changed everything.

Rehab.

The place where I faced myself.
The place where I made an impact.
The place where someone finally said:

"You don't belong here forever.
You actually want to be better."

I didn't walk into rehab ready to heal.
I walked into **prison.**

Because this wasn't a facility.
It wasn't a clinic.
It wasn't a place for therapy or care.

It was **SAF-P** —
a "rehabilitation program" run on prison grounds
with concrete floors, steel doors,
and guards who carried shotguns
instead of compassion.

They stripped me of my name the moment I arrived.
Not literally —
spiritually.

When I stepped off the bus,
still wearing my golds,
still looking like the world I came from,

an old white guard scanned me from head to toe
and asked:

"What *hood* are you from?"

Just like that.
Labeled.
Reduced.
Dismissed.
Before I even breathed the air inside.

He smirked, like he already knew my story.
Like I was the reason he hated his job.
Like I was already guilty of crimes I hadn't committed.

That same guard would later try to get me kicked out of the program
and sent straight to prison
over a lie that couldn't be proven.

They didn't care about truth.
They cared about control.

On the first day, they assigned jobs.
Some men cleaned.
Some cooked.
Some scrubbed toilets.

Mine was **garden keeper.**

I walked outside looking for direction.
A guard stood there, holding a shotgun so casually
you'd think it was part of his uniform.

I asked him what he wanted me to do.

Without looking up, he pointed at the field and said:

"Get out there and hoe with the rest of them hoes."

For a moment, I didn't even move.
Not because I was scared —
but because I was stunned.

This was "rehabilitation"?
This was "help"?
This was how they expected people to change?

By breaking them harder?

We weren't inmates.
We weren't patients.
We weren't men.

We were **numbers.**
Bodies.
Rows in a system that didn't care if we ever stood up again.

And that's what I told the counselor.

One day in our session,
she expected the usual story —
the excuses, the half-lies, the empty promises.

But when I spoke,
I didn't give her a performance.

I gave her truth:

I told her they were so busy enforcing rules
they forgot they were dealing with souls.
I told her half the men in that room
would leave this program and relapse
not because they were weak,
but because nobody taught them how to cope —
they just threw them into more trauma
and called it "help."

I told her this place didn't heal people.
It **broke them better.**

When I finished,
I looked up expecting anger.

But her eyes were full.

She cried.

Right there.
In front of everyone.

And the next day?

She didn't come back.

Word spread fast:

"She quit.
Said something the kid said opened her eyes."

I had never changed a life before.
Not one that mattered.
Not on purpose.

But in that moment, something shifted.

Not in them —
in *me*.

The guards noticed.
Maybe they felt threatened.
Maybe they hated that a "number" had something to say.

They tried breaking me.

Phone calls? Gone.
Recreation? Gone.

Commissary? Gone.
Books? Gone.

They took everything they could take
short of my breath.

They wanted to silence the voice they couldn't control.

But I reached out anyway —
through letters, through whispers, through whatever channel I found.

My mother got involved —
and no matter how hard our history was,
one thing has always been true:

When it came to fighting for me,
she was a soldier.

She contacted the prison board.
And the guards hated it.

Hated me.

Hated that I wasn't breaking the way they wanted.

They watched me like a hawk.
Waited for me to slip.
Tried to corner me with accusations.
Tried to make me fold.

Months passed.

One afternoon, a guard walked up to me,
smirking like the devil just told him a joke.

"How you holding up?"
He laughed after he said it.

I looked him dead in the eyes and told him:

"You can take everything from me,
but you can't take my mind."

He stopped smiling.

Because in that moment,
he realized the truth:

I wasn't the prisoner.

He was.

As the months went on,
something strange happened.

People — inmates — started coming to me.

For advice.
For clarity.
For comfort.
For understanding.

Older women.
Hard women.
Women who never opened up to anybody.

But they opened up to me.

Something about the way I talked.
The honesty.
The insight.
The heart.

Something they weren't used to hearing
from someone like me.

I wasn't trying to be a leader.
But leadership found me anyway.

And before long,
I was changing people from the inside
in the one place meant to strip you of your insides completely.

When I completed the program,
they gave me a certificate.

Everyone gets one.

But they gave me **another** one.

Special.
Separate.

For impact.
For influence.
For awakening something in people
that most men never even find in themselves.

I didn't walk out healed.

But I walked out aware.

Awareness is the first step
toward becoming the man
I was always meant to be.

Rehab didn't fix me.

It introduced me
to myself.

The version of me
that trauma tried to kill
but purpose refused to let die.

Walking out of SAF-P didn't feel like freedom.
It felt like stepping into a world that was still on fire,
and now I could finally *see* the flames.

Rehab on prison grounds had stripped me down.
Not in the way the guards wanted —
not into nothing —

but into **someone.**

Someone sharper.
Someone aware.
Someone who couldn't pretend anymore.

But the world I came back to?
It wasn't ready for the version of me that walked out.

My mother picked me up that day.

And every mile felt like a reminder
that this homecoming wasn't a celebration —
it was a return to unfinished business.

When we got home, the house felt the same:
loud, disorganized, tense, heavy.
Trauma doesn't redecorate just because you do.

The boys were older.
Bigger.
But the energy was familiar:
quiet, watchful, fragile.

I remember sitting in my old room,
the walls too close,
the ceiling too low,
and thinking:

"I left this place broken.
I came back aware.
But everything around me stayed the same."

And that's when I realized something painful:

Awareness doesn't heal you.
It just makes dysfunction impossible to ignore.

I tried to walk with new habits.
New perspective.
New discipline.

I tried to breathe differently,
talk differently,
move differently.

But trauma has muscle memory.

The smell of the house.
The way my mother spoke.
The tone in her voice.
The chaos in the environment—

all of it tugged at the old version of me
like it wanted him back.

And I could feel the war inside:

the man I found in rehab
vs.
the kid this house created.

They didn't know each other.
They didn't trust each other.
They didn't speak the same language.

And I was caught in the middle.

I reached out to Mariah again.
I couldn't help it.

She had been my anchor
long before I knew what anchors were.

We talked slowly at first.
Cautiously.
Like people who still loved each other
but had learned to be afraid of what that love could cost.

She'd always believed in me,
even when I didn't.

But now she didn't know who I was anymore —
and truthfully, neither did I.

I wanted to tell her everything I'd realized.
Everything I'd changed.
Everything I wanted to be.

But healing has a timing.
And mine was still fragile —
too fragile to hand to someone else.

So I didn't say the things I should have.
Didn't apologize the way I owed her.
Didn't express what was breaking me open from the inside.

I just hoped she could feel it.

Hoped she saw the man I was trying to become
instead of the boy I had been.

But the hardest part?

Looking in the mirror.

Because for the first time,
I knew exactly who I *didn't* want to be —
and I wasn't fully sure how to become
the man I knew I could be.

Awareness is a blessing.
But at first, it feels like a curse.

It shows you the gap
between your intentions
and your habits,
between your dreams
and your past,
between who you are
and who you're afraid you might always be.

I stood there,
staring at my own reflection,
and whispered to myself:

"You survived.
Now you gotta learn how to live."

That was the real rehab.

Not SAF-P.
Not the certificate.
Not the counselors.

This.
This moment.

The moment when running wasn't an option anymore.
The moment I had to face myself
with no substances,
no distractions,

no street persona,
no masks.

Just me.

And the mirror.

Chapter 9

"Relapse, Willie, and Thirteen Months"

When I walked out of rehab,
I thought the hardest part of my life was behind me.

I was wrong.

Sometimes the real battle starts
after the war.

Mariah wanted clarity.

Not drama.
Not chaos.
Just truth.

She sat across from me not long after I got out—
not angry,
not demanding,
just trying to understand where we stood.

She asked me straight:

"How do you want to move forward… with us?"

And I froze.

Not because I didn't love her.
I did.

Deeply.
Unshakably.

But in rehab, they drilled something into us:

Recovery is selfish.

You have to choose yourself so fiercely
that everything else comes second.
Even the person you love most.

So I told her I needed to work on myself.

It was honest.
But honesty doesn't always feel like love.

So she made a choice.

Someone else had been pursuing her.
Stable.
Military.
Structured.

Everything I wasn't at the time.

She moved forward.

And in my insecurity,
my fear,
my wounded pride,
I moved forward with someone else too.

She got engaged.
So did I.

But the difference?

She was trying to build a life.
I was still trying to outrun mine.

She settled into stability.
I spiraled quietly under the surface—
running on substances, survival instincts, and denial.

My mom even asked:

"Do you want to go to her wedding?"

I said no.

Not because I didn't care.
Because I cared too much.

I couldn't handle the truth:

I was losing her again—
this time, not because of what was done to us,
but because of who I wasn't ready to become.

Relapse in Slow Motion

I relapsed.

Not all at once.
Not with a dramatic crash.

Slow.

I was working nights.
Exhausted.
Trying to grind my way into a new life.

So I took pills to stay awake,
to stay alert,
to stay "functional."

I'd stopped smoking weed.
Stopped doing booger sugar.

I told myself pills were "milder."
Just temporary.
Just to cope.
Just to get through this season.

But addiction doesn't negotiate.
It waits.

And even inside that relapse,
I still had ambition.

I wanted to be a Licensed Chemical Dependency Counselor.

I wanted to help other people heal.
Use my story to save lives.
Be the person I never had.

I started outpatient treatment.
I was actually doing well.
For the first time, I could almost see a future
that wasn't built on chaos.

Then came the call.

Willie Goes Missing

Willie was missing.

My best friend.
My brother in spirit.
Schizophrenic.
Unpredictable.
Hurting in ways most people never try to understand.

His mom called and asked if I'd seen him.

I hadn't.

Days passed. No word.

My spirit got loud:

"Go find him."

So I did.

I grabbed my keys and, for some reason,
decided to take my Mercedes
deep into a neighborhood
where it did not belong.

Willie's younger brother came with me.

I didn't know he had a gun.

I didn't know that trying to help
was about to cost me everything.

The police pulled us over.

They saw the gun.

In that split second,
I saw my entire future hanging by a thread.

I had been trying to get it right this time.
Going to treatment.
Showing up.
Doing the work.

And now this.

I knew what they would assume.
What they would write.
What they would charge.

I knew prison was waiting
on the other side of that discovery.

I panicked.
And I ran.

Not because I didn't want accountability.

Because I was terrified
that I was about to lose the little bit of future
I had barely begun to build.

I didn't get away.

They caught me.

I can admit now it was a wakeup call.

The system never cares why you run.
Only that you did.

I fought for freedom for 13 months.

Thirteen months for trying to check on a missing friend.
Thirteen months for a gun that wasn't mine.
Thirteen months for a relapse I never wanted
and a life I was trying to fix
but didn't yet know how to hold together.

It wasn't fair.
But it was real, real that I realized I was being saved from myself again.

And it changed everything.

Classroom in a Cage

I refused to waste that time.

I picked up real books:

Think & Grow Rich.
The Four Agreements.
The Education of Millionaires.

I took notes.
Studied myself.
Studied the world.
Studied possibility.

I poured what I learned into the people around me.

I encouraged them.
Spoke about purpose.
About healing.
About breaking cycles.

But not everyone likes light in dark places.

One morning,
darkness answered back.

Twenty Against One

The first hit came from behind.

My ears rang.
Vision blurred.

By the time I turned,
they were everywhere.

Fists.
Feet.
Shoes.
Knees.

Stomping.
Kicking.
Punching.

Some of the faces
were the same ones I had fed,
encouraged,
and spoken life into.

That's the thing about survival zones:
loyalty doesn't live there.
Fear does.

Instinct told me to fight back.
Spirit told me something else.

I dropped to the ground
and protected my neck.

Then I did something
that looked like giving up from the outside
but was actually the most powerful thing I could do:

I went still.

Completely still.

And I prayed.

Not for revenge.
Not even for rescue.

I prayed for peace.
For protection.
For breath.

If they were going to kill me,
I didn't want to die fighting my own fear.

I wanted to die in surrender—
knowing I'd finally stopped fighting myself.

The hits finally stopped.

Silence came back in pieces.

When I tried to move my fingers
and they responded,
when my toes answered back,
when breath filled my lungs—

I realized I had survived something
most men don't walk away from.

Solitary and a Dying Grandmother

They put me in solitary "for safety."

But solitary isn't safety.

It's a coffin you're forced to live in
with your eyes open.

Twenty-three hours a day
in a concrete box
with nothing but my thoughts
and the sound of my own breathing.

No explanations.
No closure.
Just echo.

Then came a phone call.

My grandmother was dying.

"Only a few weeks to live," they said.

It felt like someone reached through the phone
and crushed my chest from the inside.

I loved her more than most people know.
Her hands, her voice, her spirit
had been one of the few gentle things in my childhood.

And now, while I sat in a cement cell,
she was fading.

I prayed harder in that box
than I ever had in my life.

They said she had weeks.

She's still here.

Some souls refuse to leave
before their descendants become
who they're meant to be.

I spent Christmas in solitary.

No tree.
No music.
No warmth.

Just four walls
and a future I had no map for.

But again, something happened in there
that no rehab, no jail, no street ever gave me, it came from within:

I grew.

Back With Her, Still Building Me

By then, Mariah had moved to Atlanta
with her "fake fiancé."

We both knew that wedding
was never going to happen.

She didn't go through with it.

We found our way back to each other—
again.

We got back together when I was released.
Moved into an apartment in Houston.

It was rough.

Two people with history, trauma, triggers, anger, and love,
trying to build something in a world
that had never handed either of us a blueprint.

I was learning how to control:

my emotions,
my reactions,
my mind.

She was learning how to trust again.
How to love someone
who was still under construction.

It wasn't pretty.

But it was real.

And we were willing
to work through it together.

The First Big Dream Blocked

Getting out after 13 months,
I felt different.

Not triumphant.
Not rebellious.

Grounded.

I knew exactly what I wanted:

To help people.
To be the counselor I never had.
To become a Licensed Chemical Dependency Counselor—an LCDC.

I took action this time and threw myself into school.

Showed up early.
Took notes.
Listened hard.

I wasn't just studying.
I was building a life.

I was good at it.

I understood addiction
from the inside out.

When practicum time came,
everyone else in the program
got placements.

I got doors closed.

One after another:

"We're sorry.
With your background, we can't accept you."

Not because I was unqualified.
Not because I was unprepared.

Because of who I used to be.

I was almost finished.
Almost credentialed.
Almost ready to launch a career
that could have helped thousands.

Almost.

"Almost" is a knife
when you're trying to escape your past.

Eventually, the program director sat me down.

She wasn't cruel.
She was honest.

"I'm sorry.
You won't be able to complete your hours.
No facility will accept your record."

Just like that:

A year of effort.
A year of hope.
A year of doing everything right—

Gone.

I walked out of that office
feeling like the universe was mocking me.

Not because I wasn't good enough.
Because the world refused to believe
I could be something other than my past.

So I did the only thing
that made sense in that moment:

I started working out.

Heavier.
Harder.
Longer.

Because weights were the only thing in my life
that moved when I pushed.

If I lifted, it rose.
If I strained, it grew.

People noticed.

"You ever thought about being a personal trainer?"

I had.

I thought about life coaching too.

But every time I tried to dream,
I could feel all the shut doors behind me.

I wasn't lost.

I was blocked.

And even then, another collision
was already on its way.

Literally.

Chapter 10

"Two Wrecks: Blindness"

The first crash
didn't come from recklessness.

It came from family.

From reaching across decades of distance,
trying to reconnect with the people
who shared my father's blood.

The First Wreck: Blindness

I hadn't seen my father's family
since I was around ten.

Eighteen years.

Almost two decades of silence and wondering.

After everything I'd survived—
rehab, jail, heartbreak,
blocked opportunities—

I felt a pull toward them.

So that Thanksgiving,
I went.

I visited my father's grave.
Stood over the man whose death
had rewired my entire life at age six.

Then I went to my grandmother's house.

Her.
My uncles.
My cousins.

My father's people.
My people.

We laughed.
Talked.

Tried to stuff nearly two decades
into a few hours.

For the first time in a long time,
I didn't feel like a survivor.

I finally felt normal.

Later that day,
one of my cousins said she needed to pick up her son from school.

"Let me ride," I said.

She said yes.

It was dark outside.

The only real light
came from the stadium near the school.

We drove, talking,
wrapped in that deep country night.

Then—

A firecracker exploded in the sky.

Harmless celebration.
Wrong place, wrong time.

An older man driving a white Mustang
heard it.

It startled him so badly
he went into cardiac arrest
right there behind the wheel.

His foot hit the gas—
dead weight.

His car veered,
crossed the line,
and slammed head-on into ours.

Metal.
Sound.
Silence.

Everything went black.

When I opened my eyes,
it wasn't night.

It was blindness.

I was blind
for two months.

Two months inside my own head.
Two months wondering if sight
was something I'd only ever have in my memories.

The man in the Mustang died.

We lived.

I still don't fully understand why.

That first wreck
wasn't a punishment.

It was a collision of fate—

I didn't know it then,
but that crash was a prelude.

The universe wasn't done with me yet.

Chapter 11

"The Motorcycle, the Metal, and the Man I Became"

Before the second crash,
I wasn't running.

But I was chasing.

Chasing money.
Chasing stability.
Chasing something I could point to and say,
"See? I made it."

I was working fire inspections that day.

I was supposed to stay at the site
until the extinguishers were checked.

But I knew once the inspector left,
the door would lock.

And my mind was on one thing:

Beat Houston traffic.

Downtown at rush hour—
even on a motorcycle—
is its own kind of punishment.

I wanted to get home.

And home
wasn't just an apartment.

It was a manifestation.

Months earlier,
I was DoorDashing when I delivered to a building
I had no business walking into.

Twenty-three stories.
Concierge.
Luxury lobby.
Soft lighting.

The kind of place I never imagined for someone
with my record, my scars, my past.

Then the elevator opened.

Houston's skyline poured into my chest.

For a moment, I was quiet.

Then my spirit said:

"You're going to live here."

Immediately, doubt snapped back:

"People like you don't live in places like this. Be serious."

But for the first time in my life,
I didn't just swallow that voice.

I argued with it.

"Why not?"

I delivered the food,
walked back out,
looked up at that glass tower and said:

"I'll be home later."

Less than six months later,
I was living there.

The Call Before Impact

The day of the wreck felt regular.

Too regular.

I'd left the work site early,
thinking about nothing more serious than traffic and dinner.

I called Mariah.

"I'll be home soon," I told her.

"I'm making burgers," she said.

Normal.
Soft.
Simple.

I hung up,
pulled into the street,
caught a red light.

It turned green.

I rolled forward—maybe 30 mph.

Then a car turned in front of me.
Sideways.
And stopped.

No time to swerve.
No time to think.

Just enough time to know:

"This is going to be bad."

I told myself:

"You're going to be okay."

Then I braced.

Impact.

My body hit the car.
Then the pavement.
Then air.
Then pavement again.

I bounced.
Rolled.
Skidded.

When I finally stopped moving,
I was on my back in the street,
staring at a sky that didn't make sense.

But I was conscious.

Alive.

Somehow.

The driver ran over,
apologizing.

"I didn't see you," he kept saying.

Later he'd tell the police it was my fault.

But in that moment,
we both knew the truth.

Witnesses circled.

One man—
a lifelong biker—
knelt beside me.

Later he told me
he'd been riding for thirty years.

After seeing what I survived,
he'd never ride again.

The first thing I asked the crowd was:

"Call my mom."

Shock is a strange mercy.
Pain hadn't landed yet.

I couldn't lift my legs.
One arm was clearly broken.

When the paramedics arrived,
I asked one of them to take a picture.

Because even at the edge of death,
humor was still the armor I knew how to reach for.

Then they cut my clothes off.

And everything changed.

Bleeding From the Inside

They saw my stomach swelling.

Internal bleeding.

The same thing that killed my father.

Their faces shifted from "accident"
to "fight for his life."

They pressed down
to keep my organs together.

That pain—
I had never known anything like it.

I wailed.

A paramedic spoke to my mom over the phone,
trying to calm her:

"If he can feel this much pain," she said,
"it means he's alive. It means he isn't paralyzed."

Even in all that agony,
I felt a flicker of gratitude.

I asked the paramedic:

"Am I going to die?"

She didn't answer.

And sometimes, silence
is louder than any truth.

Rebuilt Out of Metal

At the hospital,
the truth came in waves:

Both arms—broken.
Pelvis—shattered.

Not a small fracture.
Not a clean break.

A collapse.

It took 5 surgeries in 2 days,
8 rods,
26 screws
to put me back together.

Two broken arms.
A broken pelvis.
A catheter.
Immobilized legs.

My father had died from internal bleeding
after a crash.

I survived the same.

This wreck didn't just injure me.
It rewrote me.

When I finally woke up enough
to understand what happened,

I knew:

My father's death
was not my destiny.

His story ended on the pavement.

Mine restarted there.

Broken.
Humbled.
Reborn.

The Christmas I Shouldn't Have Made It Home

The wreck was on December 12, 2022.
Thirteen days before Christmas.

I didn't want my family
spending another holiday in a hospital because of me.

After everything I'd already put them through—
arrests, hearings, phone calls from cells—

I refused to make Christmas
another chapter in that book.

The doctors expected me to stay.
Longer.

They didn't think I'd be
walking
anytime soon.

But I made myself a promise:

"I will be home by Christmas."

About five days in,
the physical therapist came in all business.

"If you can get from the bed
to the bedside toilet
on your own
once we remove the catheter—
we can talk discharge."

Two broken arms.
A shattered pelvis.
Pain that lit up my whole body.

It sounded impossible.

But I had something stronger than pain:

Purpose.

I pushed myself
harder than I ever had.

Lowered myself off the bed.
Gripped the walker with broken arms.
Inched my way toward that toilet.

Every movement felt like fire.

But I did it.

Barely.
But I did.

That was enough.

December 22, 2022—
ten days after the crash—
they discharged me.

They loaded me into an ambulance,
brought me up the freight elevator
of the same high-rise I had once manifested in a daydream.

A hospital bed waited in my living room,
right where the skyline used to make me feel invincible.

Now it made me feel small.
Human.
Grateful.

Alive.

When Mariah Became My Body

At home,
I couldn't do anything by myself.

Not eat.
Not bathe.
Not dress.
Not stand.
Not get to the bathroom.

My body had become a prison again.

But Mariah—
she became my body
while mine remembered how to work.

She took leave from her job.
No hesitation.

She fed me.
Wiped me.
Changed me.
Lifted me in and out of wheelchairs.
Got me to every appointment.
Every scan.
Every physical therapy session.

She carried me
back into life.

And when I didn't want life for myself,
she spoke it back into me.

There is no greater love than that.

Becoming Myself, Not Someone Else

I didn't wake up from the wreck and say,

"I want to become a man."

That's not my story.

The truth was quieter.

I had always been me.
Long before I had language for it.
Long before the world had options for it.
Long before my mother tried to beat it out of me
or the church tried to pray it away.

The wreck didn't create who I am.

It stripped away everything I was pretending to be.

When your body is forced into stillness—
when you can't move, can't run, can't distract—

your spirit gets louder.

All I had was:

My mind.
My memories.
My truth.

The realization wasn't dramatic.

No fireworks.
No single epiphany.

Just a quiet alignment:

My body,
my reflection,
my voice,
my spirit

had never been in agreement.

Not because something was "wrong."

Because it wasn't mine.

I didn't want to become someone new.

I wanted to stop betraying who I'd always been.

My Mother's Unexpected Grace

My mother had already accepted my sexuality
long before the wreck.

What surprised me
was what came after.

We'd had deep conversations.
Hard ones.

She told me she had been young,
stressed,
grieving my father,
alone,
and drowning
when she was raising us.

That she didn't have the tools.
Didn't have support.
Didn't have healing.

And that she had projected her pain onto me.

She apologized.

For real.
No excuses.

Then, when it came time for my surgery,
she did something
that still humbles me:

She paid.

Maybe it was guilt.
Maybe it was love.
Maybe it was her way of saying:

"I couldn't protect you then.
But I can support you now."

Paying for that surgery
wasn't about "making me" anything.

It was her helping me
honor who I already was.

Her way of saying:

"I see you now.
I'm sorry.
And I'm trying."

And for me,
after everything we'd survived together and against each other—
that mattered.

Transition didn't turn me into someone else.

It let me finally live as myself
without apology.

The wreck almost took my life.

Recovery gave me back
the one I actually wanted.

Chapter 12

"The Long Road Back to Purpose"

Healing didn't hand me a straight line.

It handed me a maze.

After the wreck,
after the surgeries,
after the transition,
after learning to walk again—

life didn't magically fall into place.

If anything, it felt like the universe said:

"Now that you're alive,
let's see what you're made of."

Attempt #1: The Counselor I Needed

Right after those 13 months locked up—
before the wreck ever happened—
I had enrolled in school
to become an LCDC.

A Licensed Chemical Dependency Counselor.

I wanted to be what I never had.

I was almost done.

Then practicum time came
and every door closed.

Not because I wasn't capable.
Because of my background.

"We're sorry.
With your record, we can't take you."

Over and over.

A career that fit my heart
was blocked by my past.

Attempt #2: The Body Dream

After that, I threw myself into fitness.

Lifting felt like the only space in my life
where effort = results.

Somebody told me:

"You should be a trainer."

It made sense.

Then the second wreck hit.

Eight rods.
Twenty-six screws.
Broken arms.
Broken pelvis.

Personal training, at least in that season,
was gone before I could fully build it.

Attempt #3: Deals and Documents

Before I was even fully out of the wheelchair,
I was back at work.

Not lifting.
Not standing on my feet all day.

Thinking.

I got a job in an office,
brokering businesses.

Mergers & acquisitions.
Deals.
Numbers.
Contracts.

I became an ABI—
an Accredited Business Intermediary.

And I was good at it.

But the fit wasn't right.
The season ended.

But my efforts weren't paying off.

Attempt #4: Breaking My Body for a Paycheck

Next came a warehouse job.

Hard.
Heavy.
Physical.

My body wasn't fully healed,
but I worked anyway.

I went from temp
to associate
to lead
in a matter of months.

When you've fought for survival your whole life,
you don't show up halfway.

But killing your body for a paycheck
isn't purpose.

It's desperation with direct deposit.

Attempt #5: The Lie That Looked Like a Ladder

Then came the company that promised:

"Family."
"Freedom."
"Opportunity."

It was a pyramid scheme.

And like all good scams,
it fed on hunger and hope.

I lost my job.
Lost my focus.
Almost lost my relationship.

Mariah saw it first.

She saw the obsession.
The emotional distance.
The way our home started to feel
like a staging ground
for someone else's dream.

She tried to warn me.

Eventually, I realized:

I was being used.

I left.
Unpaid.
Unappreciated.
Angry—

but standing up for myself.

That exit cost me money,
but it restored my integrity.

It reminded me:

I had spent too much of my life
letting other people decide my worth.

That season was over.

Turning Down the "Dream" Offer

Then came the job search.

Applications.
Interviews.
Silence.

Until a six-figure offer came.

The kind of offer
someone with my background
is "supposed" to grab without thinking.

But I had learned the difference
between alignment and temptation.

And something in my spirit said:

"This isn't it."

So I turned it down.

Not because I didn't need the money.
Not because I wasn't scared.
But because I knew:

If I said yes to the wrong thing again,
I'd lose myself
all over.

For the first time,
I chose purpose
over survival.

Letting Go to Grow

Mariah and I separated.

Not because we stopped loving each other.
Because I needed to get stable.
For real.

Sometimes love chooses space
so the future version of both people
has a chance to exist.

I moved to Dallas.

Not to run away—
but to walk toward something.

I just didn't know exactly what yet.

Chapter 13

"Dallas, The Village, and Alignment"

By the time I got to Dallas,
I had crossed an invisible threshold.

For almost two months,
I had been in deep meditation.

Not the "ten minutes on an app" kind.

The kind where you sit with yourself
long enough
to meet the you
underneath the trauma,
the anger,

the labels,
the survival mode.

My transformation this time
wasn't physical.

It was spiritual.

For the first time in my life,
I felt aligned with something bigger than fear,
bigger than my record,
bigger than my past.

The universe and I were in rhythm—
quiet signs,
synchronicities,
conversations that arrived exactly on time.

I didn't doubt myself.
Didn't doubt my path.
Didn't doubt my future.

I realized:

I had finally become the version of me
I had always wanted to be.

Not perfect.
But peaceful.
Not finished.
But clear.

When I arrived in Dallas,
I wasn't running from anything.

I was walking into purpose.

The Mentors

Then the mentors came.

They didn't show up as saviors.
Or as some big "answer."

They showed up as confirmation.

Two mentors—
both connected to my extended circle
long before I ever knew them.

People who had walked their own hard roads.
People who carried integrity.
People who saw my vision
instead of my background.

They didn't look at me
and see "felon," "statistic," "project."

They saw a leader.

Without even trying,
they helped pull me out
of the last threads of survival mode.

They didn't try to rescue me.
They built with me.

In their presence,
purpose didn't feel like a dream.

It felt inevitable.

The Village

In Dallas, doors didn't just open.
They turned into hallways.

Those hallways led to:

The Village app

The Village Foundation (my nonprofit in process)

An internship under my mentor at a nonprofit

A real blueprint for my life's work

Everything I'd survived
suddenly made sense.

All the versions of me—

the hungry kid,

the angry teen,

the hurt addict,

the inmate,

the fighter,

the dreamer—

finally came together around one truth:

I am here to build what I never had.

A place for the kids like me.
A system for the families like mine.
A path for the ones everyone calls "lost"
when really, they've just never had a map.

A bridge between pain and possibility.

And Guess What?

I wrote a book.

This one.

I didn't outline it ahead of time.
Life outlined it for me.

Every arrest.
Every move.
Every loss.
Every love.
Every wreck.
Every prayer.
Every relapse.
Every second chance.

All of it wrote this
long before I ever typed it.

So to you—
the reader,
the survivor,
the struggler,
the one who doesn't know how to start over:

Be inspired by my story.
Be resilient.
Stop just living—
and start experiencing life.

This isn't the end.

This is the beginning
of everything I was born to build.

And maybe,
if you let it,
it's the beginning of something new in you, too.

Chapter 14:

"What I Want You to Know About Your Own Life"

If you're holding this book,
there's a reason.

Maybe you're hurting.
Maybe you're searching.
Maybe you're surviving more than living.
Maybe you feel alone,
or misunderstood,
or tired in a way sleep can't fix.

Or maybe you're like I was —
holding the pieces of a life
no one taught you how to survive
and wondering why the hell you're still here.

Let's talk.

Not as author to reader.

But as one soul to another.

1. Your story doesn't have to start pretty to end powerful.

We don't get to choose how our story starts.
We don't choose the parents,
the neighborhoods,
the trauma,
the losses,
the addictions,
the bad decisions,
the heartbreaks.

But we do get to decide what the story becomes.

People like us don't get easy beginnings.

But we get meaningful endings.

And meaningful endings always start with one choice:

Refuse to let the beginning define you.

2. Pain doesn't make you weak.

It makes you awake.

People think strength is about never breaking.

But the strongest people I know
are the ones who broke
again
and again
and again
and still showed up for life
when everything in them said stay down.

I used to be ashamed of my past.
Ashamed of my trauma.
Ashamed of my addictions.
Ashamed of my records.
Ashamed of how long it took me
to understand myself.

Now I realize something:

Pain didn't ruin me.

Pain introduced me to myself.

3. You're not behind.

You're being prepared.

Read that again.

I spent years thinking:

"I should've been further by now."
"I should've had more."
"I should've been stable."
"I should've been healed."
"I should've been better."

But every delay was a detour
that saved my life.

Every closed door
was protection.

Every heartbreak
was redirection.

Every failure
was a lesson disguised as loss.

You are not late.
You are not slow.
You are not stuck.

You are in process.

And process takes time.

4. *You don't have to earn your worth.*

You already have it.

Read that slowly.

I spent my whole life trying to earn worth
from people who couldn't give it to me.
Trying to win love

from people who didn't know how to love themselves.
Trying to prove value
to a world that only saw my mistakes.

You don't have to prove anything.

You don't have to achieve your way into being valuable.
You don't have to survive your way into being lovable.
You don't have to become "successful"
to matter.

You matter
because you exist.
Period.

5. *Forgiveness is not for them.*

It's for you.

This one took me years.

Forgiving my mother
didn't erase the things she did.
Forgiving the cops
didn't erase the beatings.
Forgiving the people who hurt me
didn't unhurt me.

Forgiveness isn't approval.

It's release.

It's choosing not to bleed from the same wound forever.

It's letting your story grow past the pain
that started it.

You deserve that peace.
Even if the people who hurt you
never offer closure.

6. Your past is not a prison sentence.

It's a passport.

My record said "felon."
People said "failure waiting to happen."
My life said I should be dead,
locked up,
lost,
or forgotten.

And yet —
here I am.

Not because the past disappeared.

But because I turned it into purpose.

Your past is not a barrier.
It's a blueprint.

A roadmap.
A resource.
A story only you can translate.

There are people waiting to be changed
by the very things you're ashamed to talk about.

What broke you
will build someone else.

Don't waste it.

7. You don't need the world's permission

to become who you truly are.

Becoming myself
wasn't about labels,
or categories.

It was about truth.

It was about finally choosing the life
that honored my spirit
instead of suffocating it.

You don't have to fit inside anyone's understanding
to deserve authenticity.

Be who you are
before the world tells you who to be.

You owe them nothing.

You owe you everything.

8. Love is healing when it is chosen,

not when it is begged for.

Mariah loved me through my darkest hours.
She cared for me when I couldn't care for myself.
She saw the parts of me
I was afraid to face.

But even with love that deep,
even with history,
even with destiny —

we had to separate
so we could grow.

Love is not possession.
Love is not dependency.
Love is not survival.

Love is choosing each other
when you're whole enough
to give something real.

Love is coming back stronger —
not staying while broken.

9. *Purpose isn't something you find.*

It's something you become.

For years I chased purpose.
Through jobs,
through schemes,
through school,
through hustle,
through desperation.

Purpose didn't show up
until I stopped running,
until I healed,
until I listened.

Purpose comes when you're ready to stop surviving
and start serving.

Everything I lived
— every wreck,
every trauma,
every heartbreak,
every relapse,
every detour —
wasn't punishment.

It was preparation.

Preparation for the Village.
Preparation for mentorship.
Preparation for leadership.
Preparation for the people
I'm called to lift.

And preparation for you
to find your own path through my story.

10. Your life is not over.

Not even close.

If you take nothing else from my story,
take this:

You have more chapters left.
More purpose left.
More love left.
More healing left.
More laughter left.
More life left.

You are not done.
I don't care what you've survived.
I don't care what you've lost.
I don't care how many mistakes you've made.
I don't care how old you are
or how damaged you feel
or how hopeless you think you've become.

As long as there is breath in your body —
your story is still unfolding.

And it can become something
more beautiful
more powerful
more meaningful
than anything you've experienced so far.

I'm living proof.

And now —
you are too.

The Last Words I Leave With You

Stop surviving your life.
Start experiencing it.

You deserve joy.
You deserve peace.
You deserve healing.
You deserve love.
You deserve purpose.
You deserve to see yourself
the way the universe sees you:

Not broken —

Becoming.

Not lost —

Emerging.

Not late —

Right on time.

The world hasn't met the best version of you yet.

But it will.

And when it does,
your story will save someone else's life
the way mine saved yours.

The end of this book
is the beginning of your next chapter.

Epilogue:

"Purpose Isn't Something You Find — It's Something You Become."

When I look back at my life now,
I don't see tragedy.

I see training.

I don't see broken pieces.

I see building materials.

I don't see a wasted life.

I see a forged one.

Every moment that tried to end me —
the hunger,
the violence,
the instability,
the abuse,
the addictions,
the wrecks,
the jail cells,
the heartbreaks,
the losses —
all of it was shaping me
into a someone I couldn't yet imagine.

Someone with depth.
Someone with vision.

Someone with empathy.
Someone with purpose.

And purpose didn't arrive like a lightning bolt.
It didn't appear in a classroom
or a job
or a paycheck
or a title.

Purpose revealed itself slowly,
the way dawn creeps into a dark room.

Through healing.
Through stillness.
Through honesty.
Through self-respect.
Through choosing myself
instead of repeating patterns.

Purpose didn't wait for me to be perfect.

It waited for me to be ready.

Ready to release the versions of myself
that were only built for survival.

Ready to stop asking the world for permission.

Ready to stop performing for acceptance.

Ready to honor the truth
I spent years burying under pain.

Ready to live
—not just exist.

The truth is this:

Purpose isn't found in a moment.

It's lived into
through every small decision
to rise
a little higher
than your circumstances.

It's what happens
when you stop asking
"Why me?"
and start asking
"What now?"

It's the quiet courage
to turn wounds into wisdom
and scars into direction.

Purpose is the version of you
that only reveals itself
after you've survived
everything that was meant to break you.

If you are reading this,

your purpose is already calling you.

Maybe softly.
Maybe loudly.
Maybe in whispers.
Maybe in crashes.

But it's calling.

Through the things that hurt you
and the things that healed you.
Through your disappointments

and your breakthroughs.
Through your mistakes
and your moments of clarity.

Purpose has been following you
your entire life.

Now it's your turn to follow it back.

And as for me?

I'm still becoming.

Still healing.
Still growing.
Still rebuilding.
Still rising.

The Village Foundation is just beginning.
My voice is just beginning.
My leadership is just beginning.
My impact is just beginning.

I am finally living the life
I was meant to live all along —
not because I chose it perfectly
but because I survived long enough
to recognize it.

This book is not a conclusion.

It is a doorway.

A hand reached back
to anyone walking the path behind me.

A reminder that no matter who you were,
what you did,

what was done to you,
what you lost,
or how long you've been stumbling in the dark —

you are allowed to step into the light.

You are allowed to begin again.

And again.
And again.

Every day if you need to.

Your story is not over.

Neither is mine.
We're both just getting started.

Close this book,
but don't close your heart.

Close this chapter,
but don't close your hope.

Go live the life
only you can create.

And one day,
may your story reach back
and save someone else's.

Just like mine reached you.

With love,

— *Tremaine*

Acknowledgments

This book may have my name on the cover, but it is built out of the lives, love, and lessons of many people.

To my mother —

Thank you for surviving long enough to grow, to apologize, and to love me in ways neither of us were taught how to give. Your honesty and willingness to revisit the hardest parts of our story made this book possible.

To Mariah —

You have been a thread through every era of my life. From teenage whispers in church pews to hospital rooms and high-rise recovery, you have loved me when I was lost and when I started to find myself. You helped me finish what the world never thought I could even start.

To my brothers —

You were my first responsibility and my first purpose. I'm sorry for the times my pain became your storm. Thank you for your forgiveness and your growth. My hope is that our adulthood together makes up for some of what we lost in childhood.

To my grandmother —

Your presence and your stubborn love have kept you here longer than anyone expected. Knowing you were still breathing while I sat in solitary gave me one more reason to keep going.

To Willie —

My brother in spirit. We were wild, hurting, and alive together. Thank you for the laughter, the late nights, and the reminder that even in chaos, there can be real connection.

To my mentors in Dallas —

Thank you for seeing a leader in me when others only saw a record. For treating me like a partner, not a project. For making space for The Village to be born.

To every counselor, teacher, and staff member who saw more than a case number —

You may never know what your small acts of humanity did, but they helped me stay alive long enough to become this version of myself.

To the men and women I was locked up with —

You showed me how much pain is walking around this world without language, help, or hope. You are one of the reasons I will never stop building spaces for healing, honesty, and second chances.

To the kids I'm building The Village for —

I wrote this for you as much as for me. Everything I'm building now, I'm building so you don't have to break the way I did just to find yourself.

To the reader —

Thank you for trusting me with your time, your triggers, and your heart. If any part of this story helped you feel less alone, then none of what I survived was wasted.

And finally, to the God/Source/Spirit who kept breath in my lungs when cars flipped, when pills tried to take me out, and when despair sat on my chest — thank You for not letting my story end where statistics said it should.

This is not just my book. It's our record that we were here, that we hurt, that we healed, and that we became.

ABOUT THE AUTHOR

Tremaine Criner is a survivor, speaker, and community builder whose life defies every statistic meant to contain him. Raised in poverty, violence, and instability, he spent his childhood fighting to protect his brothers while carrying wounds no child should bear. By his teens, he had endured abuse, homelessness, addiction, incarceration, and the devastating loss of innocence.

But Tremaine's story didn't end in trauma—it began there.

After a near-fatal motorcycle crash that shattered his body and nearly took his life, Tremaine rebuilt himself from the inside out. He became a student of healing, identity, spirituality, and purpose. Today, he is the founder of The Village Foundation, a youth-centered movement designed to give the next generation the safety, guidance, and support he never had.

Tremaine lives by one truth:

"You can take everything from me, but you can't take my mind."

This is his first book.

If you're ready to turn your past into power and step into the next chapter of your life, you'll find more tools, stories, and guidance at:

TremaineCriner.com

Made in the USA
Coppell, TX
24 December 2025

65351380R00085